Also by Laurie Beth Jones

Jesus, CEO
The Path
Jesus in Blue Jeans

Laurie Beth Jones

Grow Something Besides Old

seeds for a joyful life

simon & schuster

SIMON & SCHUSTER
Rockefeller Center
1230 Avenue of the Americas
New York, NY 10020

Simon & Schuster and colophon are registered trademarks
of Simon & Schuster Inc.

Designed by Jeanette Olender
Illustrations by Sally Mara Sturman
Manufactured in the United States of America

10   9   8   7   6   5   4   3

Library of Congress Cataloging-in-Publication Data—
Jones, Laurie Beth
Grow Something Besides Old: seeds for a joyful life/Laurie Beth Jones
p.   cm
1. Conduct of life.   I. Title
BJ1595.J455   1998
158.1—dc21   98-34089   CIP
ISBN 0-684-83971-7

I went to talk to my mother, as is my custom when something troubles me. Pulling up a chair on the patio beside her, I said, "Mom, let's analyze this." She looked at me with kind of a sigh and a smile and said, "Honey, do me a favor this year. Don't think. Just dance."

To the Dance.

Lost in the Translation

While traveling recently in Europe I noticed a flyer posted in a hotel lobby in Lourdes, France. The rough English revealed it was a translation—perhaps from the French. Urging people to commemorate the feast day of a certain saint, the flyer described in detail the many good works this man had done to earn sainthood. In summarizing the saint's life, the translator wrote: "And after Saint Maximillian died he was immediately regretted by everyone." And so my new benediction at meetings is "May you live to be regretted by everyone."

Mine

They say that animals are here to teach us, and I learned a lesson the other day from my adopted-from-the-pound dalmatian named Lady. When I put food down for my other three dogs—all at distances several yards apart, Lady runs from bowl to bowl, chasing off the other dogs. It doesn't matter that *her* bowl is full—she still has to chase the others from theirs.

Not too long ago, I encountered a situation where pangs of jealously shot through me. I perceived someone as being more "successful" than I. Didn't God love *me* anymore?

That night as I was preparing the dogs' food I heard a Voice ask gently, "Laurie, are you going to be like Lady—chasing others from their bowls when you haven't even eaten everything in yours?"

The Gift

One of my favorite Christmas gifts is a crate of various snacks and fruit my carpenter brings by. This year in the midst of the colorful array was a big, raw, brown potato. When I asked him why the potato he said, "Just as a reminder that this is all that keeps some people from starving."

Winning

One of my personal heroes is a cowboy called "Johnny." His Cowboy Trading Post is known for miles around as a place where you can buy a horse, rent a horse, have a saddle custom made, or just sit down in the rocking chair with the calico cat in your lap and talk horses.

Recently I ordered some hay from him, and while his workers were unloading it I asked him if his racehorses were winning at the track. "Oh," he smiled, "we've gotten some great times with them. Sally is the trainer. She just passed her New Mexico trainer's test and we're proud as punch of her. Sally never really had a thing to call her own, you know," he confided. "She got pregnant at fifteen, was a mother at sixteen, and has worked real hard to find her way in the world. My wife and I took her on as our partner at the Post not too long ago, and she had such a way with trail horses we thought she might enjoy working the racehorses as well. Now you should see her," he mused, leaning back against the hay. "She carries herself so tall and proud. There's a different look in her eye." He leaned forward slightly and looked at me, saying, "Your question was, are we winning at the track? Yes, we are," he smiled. "We are definitely winning. And maybe someday the horses will come in, too."

God's goodness is never lost.
It just mostly goes
unclaimed.

My mother was sharing inspiration from a book she had recently purchased, written by Charles Reid. Its title says what I would like my life philosophy to be:

Paint what you want to see.

There is a net
under us all.
Sometimes we dance.
Sometimes we fall.
And
there is a
net
under
us all.

Proverbs Summarized

Wisdom waits early at the gate
Discipline has royal reins
Seduction is a slippery slope
and Persistence
always pays off.

I don't see prayer as being the act
of beseeching
so much as
the acknowledgment
of divine connection.

Looking Higher

I was in an ice cream store getting a chocolate yogurt snack. I noticed a three-year-old child oohing and ah-hing over a birthday cake he saw in the display case. His mother stepped behind him and lifted him up. He began to howl at the prospect of being separated from the cake before him. She said, "No, Travis, that isn't the cake we're going to have for your birthday—THIS ONE IS!" She lifted him to the highest display shelf, and there, before his eyes, was a cake even lovelier than the one he had seen before. "DINOSAURS!" he shouted in glee. "Yes, we're getting you the cake with dinosaurs on it." His mother laughed as Travis clapped his hands in delight.

I thought later: God is like that mother to us—sometimes having to lift us away from what we see and want on the *lowest* shelf to show us what He really has in mind for us—there, at the very top.

I Lost My Hat at San Simeon

My favorite hat got caught up in a gust of wind yesterday as I walked
along the pier. The wind snuck up fast and grabbed it
   and then
tossed it into the blue water where sea otters were
   playing.

This made me very sad. I'd worn that hat on picnics,
   shopping, and
on walks with laughing friends. And now it was
   gone.

As I pondered why the wind would want to steal my
   hat and throw it
into the water, a small Voice inside said, "Because the
   sea wants to play
with you." And then a darker, real mean voice said,
   "That is the
most ridiculous thing I've ever heard!"

And then the small Voice said, "God says you out-
    shine the sun . . . that
angels come to guard your steps . . . that you are far
    more precious than
the lilies of the field . . ."

And then I thought to myself, "Why *wouldn't* the
    sea want to play
with me? We are, after all, both made of water."

And it seemed the sea otters waved to me
as they dove.

Nothing can ever separate us from the
    Love of God—
except perhaps
a faulty perception
or a bad connection
or too much internal static
on the line.

I love spiders. They make a living from their innate skills and talents. If a strong wind tears their web, they simply create another one. If one of their silklike strands is damaged, they use it for nourishment.

If only we could be so creative with the strands we weave from within ourselves.

The universe is humming with creativity, and all one has to do to "get some" is ask, listen, and be ready with pen in hand.

Creativity

I awoke at dawn on Coronado beach. Out in the distance I could see fishermen casting their nets into the early morning sea. As a writer I relate to them—casting my web into a sea of gray, hoping to net something worth sharing.

The world is far too rich for me
unfolding more
than I can see—
flowers waving in the wind
tide pools breathing
out and in
a hummingbird
flit-flitting by
its ruby throat
against a sky
with clouds that billow
and recede
a yellow burst of sunflower
seeds
of beauty
everywhere
we walk.

Oh, too much talk.
Far too much talk.

I wonder what an apple feels
when it goes green to gold.
Does it sing out
"Here I'm ready!
Over here now!
Come, pick me?"
Or
does it just hang
happily
as part
of Larger Tree . . .

The ropes I've made from beauty
will soon support my swing
so I can go up higher
and take in everything.

I asked the little boy in the swing
how old he was
and he quickly
held up three fingers
and then slowly added a fourth.
"I'm three—going on four."
He jumped out of the swing,
stood up to his full height,
and said,
"See, I'm too big
to stay three
very much longer."

Baby Kisses

Sometimes I turn a corner
to behold
sunlight hitting a rose
just so
or I walk into the kitchen
to find kittens
sleeping in a drawer.

One time I discovered that Hobbs—
my cocker spaniel—
had dragged a blanket up the deck
and Jenny—the other cocker spaniel—
was using it to sunbathe.

I don't know—some call me silly

but when I see little things
like that—
that often go unnoticed—I
feel as if I'm being
kissed by God . . .

Like everywhere—
baby kisses.

A kite is joy
on a
leash.

The black bird hops between the hedges—
his long tail offering leverage
for his curious endeavors.

He's so shiny black he's purple
with eyes like bright orange beads.

The water in the birdbath
makes a perfect pool of sky.

I think of life's simplicity
when a bird like this struts by.

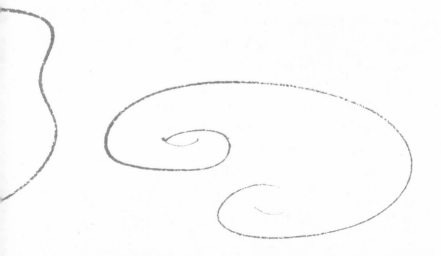

Kansas City Rose

We got on the trolley and took our seats,
interested in the driver exchange taking place
   before us.

"Bye, Rose," said the man getting off.
"Hi, Rose," said the driver getting on.
We both turned to see who Rose was.

She sat in the last wooden seat on the left,
clutching a plastic shopping bag
and wearing a painted lipstick smile
that betrayed the fact that even the mirror
was uncertain about where her lips
ended and began.

Her hair was dyed a bright, bright red
and her eyebrows too were a carefully
selected and painted-on color.
She was maybe seventy-five years old.

The trolley ride got under way and Mel and I
rode the whole circuit just to see the town.
The sun was going down and the driver turned
    and asked,
"Want to get off here, Rose?"
She said, "Yes, that will do nicely," then stepped
delicately down.

We watched her slowly walk away
along a littered sidewalk.
I asked the driver, "Does Rose ride this trolley
    every day?"
"Yes," he said. "In fact, she rides it all day
every day . . . Gets on at 8 and off at 6
just like clockwork."
"Every day?" I asked, incredulously.
"Yep. Rain or shine."
"Doesn't she have family here?"
"Just a daughter who won't speak to her.
It's kind of sad in a way. I guess we've
become her family," he said.
"We all try to look out for her.
I think her birthday was yesterday
because some of the gals bought her balloons."

"Well, thanks for the tour," I said
as we disembarked,
commenting to each other how
uncomfortable the seats were—made of wooden
    slats.

We then toured the town, went to the
NCAA finals, and sampled the famous steak houses.
But I think I will remember most
Kansas City Rose.

"How interesting," I said to Mel as we watched
Rose walk away.
"Even an old trolley car like this
has a garden
all its own."

Perspective

My friend Mary Sheldon took her eight-year-old
    niece Megan fishing with her on the Crystal Beach
    pier.
Two hours later they returned—
Mary with an exasperated look
on her face and Megan
triumphantly carrying
a bucket of minnows.
"Is that what you caught?" I laughed,
peering into the bucket.
There was a heavy sigh
as Mary said,
"I knew it was going to be a very short day
when Megan started
naming the bait."
"Oh, look, Aunt Mary," Megan shrieked,
"Fred is kissing Cynthia again!"

I want to be like my cocker spaniel puppy Nash,
because whenever he sees a sunbeam
he runs and lies down in it.

The Cat

The cat stretches and extends her claws
seducing as she takes her pause
arching and unfolding
her reverie of senses.

A taxi driver in Mexico returned a briefcase containing $33,000 in cash—tracking down the Brazilian diplomat to whom it belonged. When the grateful diplomat offered the cab driver a reward, the cabbie refused, saying, "Thank you, sir, but if I took a reward I would lose the beauty I feel inside."

Sometimes going to class
is like panning for gold—
you have to sift through a lot of gravel
before you see
a glint of shine.

Key to Success

Find a niche—
and then scratch it.

The great thing about being
a philosopher
is that you don't
really have
to do
anything.

You simply muse
on the actions
of others.

Sometimes we don't want
the Light
because we're afraid
of getting the bill.

Summer's Eve

How nice to sit
on a summer's eve
and hear the crickets
feel the breeze
look at rooftops
flanked by trees
and feel the quiet
sink to please
the deeper part
of
be-ing.

Is That a Star or a Banana?

Two hundred restless angels sat cross-legged on the gymnasium floor, adjusting their wings so as not to poke the eyes of the angel sitting next to them. The head angel had yet to arrive. He had called on his cellular phone to say that he was stuck in traffic and would be there as soon as possible. Joseph was tapping his staff impatiently on the floor, while Mary sat quietly in the Radio Flyer wagon, centered perfectly between the cardboard donkeys that had been stapled to each side. One of the sheep was busy scratching his gray felt ear, and the little duck beside him kept lifting up her duck body to study her orange webbed feet.

A woman in the audience leaned over to her husband and said, "I didn't know there were ducks at the manger." "I didn't either," he whispered, "but I'm sure the nuns should know." In front of the procession stood a child wrapped in ten yards of yellow felt. Only her eyes, her hands, and her saddle shoes were visible. All else was felt and glitter. Evidently she had been carefully instructed as to her role, as she stood very still with her arms out at a forty-five-degree angle. Above her head was a three-foot-tall "starpoint," which shook glitter on everyone around her when she sneezed. "Is that a star or a banana?" asked the same woman of her mate.

With all the angels, sheep, ducks, Joseph, Mary, wise men, and the assembled host, the gymnasium began to get very warm. Soon a buzz began from the angel section. Suddenly there was a screech of a just-turned-on microphone, and Sister Mary Margaret yelled, "Children, do you love Jesus?" One angel tilted his head as if to ask, "Is this a trick question?" Murmurs and nodding heads eventually decided that, yes, they did in fact love Jesus. "THEN BE QUIET!" she yelled at the top of her lungs, and the angels did quiet down. Just then the head angel came rushing in, took his place in front of the violin section, and the play began. A very large angel wearing Michael Jordan tennis shoes underneath his robe grabbed a megaphone and instructed all the seated angels to sing "Gloria in Excelsis." Gabriel's voice, however, had changed and descended into the lower ranges, so none of the younger angels could hit the notes, and the violins alone had to carry the tune.

During all of this, the child in yellow felt stood perfectly still, arms out at the perfect angle, doing her part to shine. Joseph, Mary, the sheep, and the other animals made their way reverentially to the stable that was in the center of the floor, and the play ended. The parents and aunts and cousins and uncles and neighbors stood and clapped and cheered.

As I was leaving, I started chuckling at that woman's question—"Is that a star or a banana?" It seemed to me to be symbolic of every major event in life. Will this event be like a star—heralding new joy and a glorious future, or will it be a banana—lying at our feet, representing only an opportunity for slipping back into the past.

Is that a star or a banana? The answer is up to each of us to decide.

My mother was coming to visit, so I hurriedly took the newly repaired vacuum cleaner and ran it through my apartment. When I was vacuuming under the bed the machine suddenly went dead. Having just spent $68 to have it repaired, I was furious. I hauled it out to my sportscar, wedged it between an open window and the front seat and drove straight back to the repair shop, where I had picked it up just days before. Brushing past several customers, I marched up to the manager and said, "I just paid a fortune to have this vacuum cleaner fixed, and now it's dead as a doornail." He apologized to his other customers for the interruption and asked, "Did you turn it over?" "Why would I do that?" I asked. "I'm not a repairman." He turned the device over and then looked up at me. "Here's your problem, Ms. Jones." He slowly pulled out a clean white pair of my underwear. Without batting an eye he whispered, "Most people prefer to pick these up by hand." Within seconds I was gone.

Flocking Birds

I have seen
ostriches standing gray and brown
with their long necks turned in one direction
and
flamingos gather silently
to stand suspended on spindled legs.
I saw three vultures
gathered once
on a fence in Texas—
in mutual agreement about an upcoming delicacy.
Pelicans
love to fly
in wave-skimming V formations . . .
I read somewhere that a child once said,
"Uh-oh, Mommy. God's birds got out!"

I sat late on my balcony
and watched high in the sky
five hawks slowly circling,
caressing the breeze.

And the thought occurred to me—
Like flocking birds—
we all need community.

Such a silly girl I've been—
trying to use my lantern
to direct
the night sky.

Stones

Lately I've felt very close to stones.
I like their sureness,
their simplicity
and their silent power.

It's almost as if each stone
is a sculpture
from God.
Just as we are, I suppose,
only the stones
a bit more sure.

Caressing the Bones

I don't know why I always cry when people sing in church. The sound of voices united, arching in praise to God never fails to move me. Perhaps it's because of my grandparents, who used to sing in the church choir, and who sat around the piano at home, teaching us harmonies to hymns. Maybe like baby elephants, I am caressing the bones.

In the fascinating book *When Elephants Weep*, the authors observed an orphaned elephant walk into a field of bones at "an elephant graveyard." This baby grabbed one of the bones in its trunk and began to caress it—waving it in the air and then holding it close to its heart.

When the authors inquired of the caretaker about the baby's behavior, he identified those particular bones as having belonged to its mother. The mother elephant had been killed by poachers and the baby was later found alone and taken to a refuge to be raised. Yet when she returned, she recognized her mother in those bleached-out bones.

I think of that baby elephant caressing the bones when something makes me cry . . . like when I was in the cathedral where Joan of Arc, my personal hero, went to have her armor blessed. I held on to the gray stone pillars, thinking of what the ceremony must have been like, and I began to weep. Later, in Rome, I went into the stone cellar that held Peter before his crucifixion. I looked at the silent gray stone walls and wondered what they must have seen and heard. What emotions did they absorb from this man who knew he was about to die— and who had lived such a glorious life. I, too, began to weep in that stone cellar prison.

I feel at these times like that baby elephant, going back through the graveyards of history clasping the bones to my heart—caressing them for what they represent to all of us—for telling us who we were—and who we may yet become.

Kim Tinkham said, "The other day my husband was musing on our front porch. He turned to me and said, 'Kim, someday I want us to own land as far as our eyes can see.'

"I patted his hand and whispered, 'Honey, at the rate our eyes are going, this will probably happen sooner than you think.'"

The Return of a Long-Ago Friend

She said, "I want to share my daughter with you
and perhaps we can go into business together."
And my heart swells up
with a long-lost joy
and I wonder
where shall I put these flowers
that so totally enhance—
and change—
my room?

Growth in You—
natural—
like green.

Love is a music box
where Truth
unwinds
in song.

I could not love you more, Dear God,
than I do right now—
this hour.

My mother is on the line,
the teakettle is on to boil
and
I could not love you more, Dear God,
than I do right now
this hour.

Begin to love
and that which is untrue in you
will dissolve and fall away.

When God made the fields full of wildflowers
the devil was so jealous
that all he could do to ruin the harmony
was to start a rumor
that one was more beautiful
than another.

When everything seems up in the air
is most when it's in
God's hands.

I think there should be
a new punctuation mark—
because some thoughts
don't just stop
on a .
And other thoughts can't quite
reach a !
And not every thought twists itself
into a ?

So I propose a new mark
for those thoughts
that curl over themselves
and move through the mind
like waves

Adult Learning

Sometimes going to class
is really about giving ourselves permission
to do, think, see, or produce
what we already know we can.

Intuition is wisdom
in retrospect.

I'd like to be
a lemonade stand
down any dusty road
God has to walk
today.

A dream is a
call
to growth.

Time Zones

At the early long-range-planning meeting
I yawned
and he said, "What time is it
where you're from?"
I said, "Two hours earlier than this."
He laughed and said,
"Well, I'm from an hour later than this."
And the thought occurred to me,
"What are we in, then?
A time warp?"
I flew two hours forward
and he flew one hour back
so we could meet
and plan the group's future—
and what is the future anyway
but time we're not really in yet.
And we both stepped out of the time
we were in
just to plan it.

Author Annie Dillard said she feels amused when she sees people wearing fashionable hats to church. She says if the Holy Spirit were really allowed to work there, people would be wearing hard hats.

We ought to be
concerned
with
doctorin'—
not
doctrine.

Lies begin as kittens—
toying with the yarn of our lives—
then grow into
the tigers
ripping out
our hearts
and eyes.

Your sins are written
in pencil.

Your prayers
in ink.

Soar on wings
made from
outstretched
hands.

Funny how a walk
around the block
can change
your mood.

Puddle splashing:
the truest way
to celebrate
the rain.

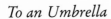

To an Umbrella

Thank you
for this
circle of dry.

A frown is a bowl of bad
just spilled.

A smile is a bowl of joy
now filled.

My ABC stands for
Ask **B**oldly **C**onstantly.

The caterpillar has 293 separate and distinct muscles in its head, while the human head encases an eight-pound organ that is mostly composed of fat.

No wonder caterpillars accomplish such amazing transformations into new life forms while we humans seem to struggle so.

As the proverb states: "You have only to will, and the power is there."

Self-Esteem

Let's face it: "The Little Engine That Could"
couldn't have
had he not summoned
some "selfish steam."

When the night is very quiet
and the air is all
a still
I can feel the eons crackle
and the paths
part to my will.

And I know
deep pooled within me
what Christ said
and Time
will prove:
If
I only look
within me
I can make
the mountains
move.

See the fruit tree
laden down
with fruit ripe for the choosing.
See the roots deep underground
that inched and crawled
round dark rocks bruising.

Faith—persistence—fruit.

Man personified the plants
as "rushes"
yet still they stand silent
at water's edge.

When Love comes looking
for the love
in you—
turn it all over.

That's all you can do.

If friend were a verb
it would be
"pour."

Sometimes I feel like sunshine must—shining on everything else that it never was.

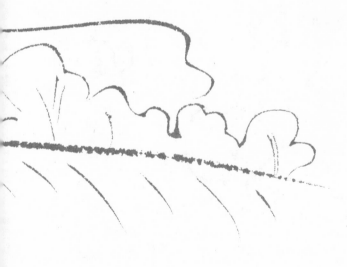

Who knows but that
the snail
was the soul
of a butterfly
that feared to stretch
dare the wind
and love.

I've never met anyone
who's been loved
enough.

Each breath was made
hesitation
until her life became
merely longing.

Love is a bubble bath
in tears.

Sometimes facing opportunity
is like staring at the knees
of a giraffe.

Q: How is a person like a safety pin?

A: It has to be open before it can be used.

If you have to watch every step you take
the path you're on
is too narrow.

Anyone can give me the money
to buy hats.
But only I can give me
the freedom
to wear them.

God, sometimes I don't need a sword
so much as
galoshes.

Love, for all its immensity,
can be measured in
the width
of a smile.

Life is entangled
in
t r **I FLE** s.

Walking through a field of sunflowers
is like having your very own
yellow eye-level parade.

Catherine's husband Ed is an avid cyclist—winning long-distance bicycle races on a consistent basis, despite his "age" of fifty-eight. After one particular victory in a sixty-mile race that took place in Juarez, Mexico, two young Mexican cyclists came up and asked Ed how old he was. Ed answered them in his best Spanish and was delighted to see them gasp and step back in awe. As he turned to smile at Catherine, she leaned over and said, "Ed, you just told them you were eighty-five years old!" "Well, you're only as old as you feel," he laughed, wiping the sweat from his brow.

I was commenting to Denny Grim, a radio talk-show host, how young he sounded on the phone, and he said, "Well, my grandkids keep me young." Then he paused and added, "It's my children that make me old."

Ten Ways to Grow Something Besides Old

1. Adopt a pet from your local animal shelter
2. Become a child advocate
3. Plan and take a trip with a friend
4. Join a choir
5. Start a walking club
6. Take a course at your local community college
7. Volunteer at a theater group
8. Read to a child every day
9. Plant a garden
10. Dance

Aging is about our spirits getting
closer to the Source
while our bodies
seem to be getting farther
from It.

After attending our mutual high school reunions,
my sister Kathy and I observed
that the beauty queens
and football heroes
now seemed like faded remnants
of their former selves,
while we (we had to admit)
had never looked or felt better.
"Well, you know what they say
on the farm," Kathy mused.
"Early bloom—
early rot."

It both saddens
and wisens me
that despite all my
wintry longings—
God never hurries
spring.

Mom and I were discussing politics.
I said, "Mom, I have observed that
a bird needs
both a right wing
and a left wing
to keep it flying."
"Yes, dear," she said, "but remember—
it's the middle
that holds everything together."

Ringed with Light

I wonder if the woman walking down the sidewalk
     today
knew she was totally ringed with light. It surrounded
her like a full-body halo. . . . as though God had
     taken a crayon
of sunbeams and outlined her head to toe.
She had her head down and was wearing a brown
knit sweater. She looked maybe sixty-five.
Probably out doing her morning walk—with tennis
shoes and all.
The sun was coming up full behind her—up over the
houses in the neighborhood.
Here it was—6:45 A.M. and this woman
was ringed
with light.

All of Life is draped in joy—
if only we could see—
the playful side of everything—
the laughter on God's knee.

Oh, yes, my eyes are laughing
delighted to be
a player in the Orchestra
and part of Harmony.

When the windows
are open
the curtains dance.

Have you ever met
stuffy people?

Nothing was ever born
in an atmosphere
of criticism—
only conformed
or destroyed.

He said, "I was a bridge for you"
his jawline all aquiver.
"Yes, you were," she calmly said.
"But I know now
I could have
swum that
river."

If you read the Bible it quickly becomes evident that most of the legendary people in it came from "dysfunctional families." Adam and Eve had one son who killed the other. Abraham and Sarah had problems with their stepchildren. King David was hated by his own son. Solomon had too many wives, and the man who helped raise Jesus was not his biological dad.

There are no formal applications
for the School of Hard Knocks
yet somehow we all
go through it—
never really having
seen the door.

We withhold from our enemies
the one thing
that would render them
our friends.

I thought my actions
most convincing
until an angel
showed me
God was wincing.

To the forest—
rain.

To the desert—
patience.

The Fragile Things

Five-year-old Megan quickly surveyed
the display of Willy's pottery.
Her eyes danced over the pots, the pouches,
the hand-woven rugs and feather red rocks
perched carefully on the glass.

Willy asked, "Megan, what do you like best
of all the things you see here?"
Megan looked up, tugged Willy's sleeve,
and said,
"I want to touch
the fragile things."

Mom called this morning at 6 A.M.
and said, "Your grandmother passed away
last night."
We knew it was coming. She was ninety-one
but the day before she was joking around—
correcting my grammar over the phone
and telling the nurses
"It sure is hard to be a princess
around this joint sometimes."

When I got off the phone
I sat by the bed and said,
"God, Life is so very frail.
I want to touch
the Fragile Things."

Ripping Apart

Do other people feel it—
this ripping of the heart
when two people separate—
one waving—
one standing still?

I watch people tear bread apart
in restaurants.
Sometimes it comes out from the kitchen
all neatly sliced
like appointments in a calendar
that are not to be debated
or discussed.
But sometimes it comes out all one loaf
and hungry hands rip it apart
and butter its jagged edges.

I am most like
unsliced bread
when it comes to you—
and the leaving of you
is a ripping apart—
a most painful
communion.

My father was always there for me when I lost.
But, then, I never really lost
when my father was there.

And the cliffs keep saying
"Nothing has changed.
Nothing has changed.
Nothing at all
has changed."

And the waves keep saying
"Everything has—
everything has—
everything
has
changed."

The Wind Chimes

The little girl sat on the concrete wall
and leaned her face against
the chain-link fence, idly fingering
the cheap white wind chimes
that were her livelihood.

Her red corduroy skirt was torn
in three places, and her purple striped sweater
had obviously belonged to someone before her.
Her face was dirty and her thick black hair was
pulled back in a loose-fitting ponytail.
She was maybe eight years old.

I asked her how much her wind chimes were
and she said without smiling
"Four dollars." I asked her if she had change
for a twenty and she said with a worried look
"No" but motioned she could get change
over there.

Meanwhile the crowd was pushing me
across the sidewalk,
eager to reach the border.

Knowing I had no time for her to get
change I gave her the three singles I had
and told her to keep the chimes.
She took the money without smiling.
It was an unsatisfactory exchange,
I knew.

How could those wind chimes ever make music
when there is no fair wind blowing—
not, at least, for the little girl
sitting on the concrete wall.

We walk across a tightrope
of hopes and dreams—
desires—
stretched across a canyon
of others' fears
and fires.

As I sat in the funeral home assisting my mother,
    brother, and sister
in making the burial arrangements for my Uncle Joe,
(the one who had killed himself)
I overheard a song in the background
playing
"Off we go
into the wild blue yonder."
Shocked, I turned to my sister and whispered,
"Did you hear that?"
and just as she turned to listen
another song came on, entitled
"I Did It My Way."

We both smiled and nodded our heads
"Yep, that's Uncle Joe all right—
trying to console us from
the grave."

There has to be a Heaven—
to be a finish to this race
to show the heart
behind the face
preserve all loveliness
like lace
reveal the constancy
of grace

There has to be a Heaven.

Death is like a train.
If you meet it going crossways
you have to stop—
no matter
who you are.

Letters wouldn't matter at all
if there weren't people
at the other end
of them.

It is no coincidence
that the eyes through which
we view life
depend on tears
to keep them
open.

When I was in grade school, my mother overheard certain kids at the playground mimicking the thick Spanish accent of one of the other students. She took us all aside and said firmly, "Whenever you hear someone speaking English with a foreign accent, remember that they speak at least one more language than you do."

I was talking with a friend about the opportunities for women entrepreneurs and about how many women still encounter discrimination at large companies. She smiled and said, "The thing I love about Heaven is that the streets are paved with gold and God has thrown out all the designs that had glass ceilings."

Recently, when I was wrestling with the direction of a creative project, Mom reminded me:

"Honey, the goal is the message—
not the market."

I think we would do better
to view reality
not as something permanent.
It is, really, you see
the petals of a flower
that exist for now—today
until God's holy breath
and will
poof them all away.

Reality?
AH-CHOO!
One sneeze
can poof
it all away.

A group I was consulting with was discussing the challenges facing a growing company. One of the topics of discussion was how much knowledge they should share, and how much they should keep to themselves.

Looking at the trends in the environment that surrounded them, one of the workers summarized the situation thusly: "It boils down to this," she said. "We either serve lunch or become lunch."

A motor-home salesman named Craig told me this story, which he claims really happened to one of his customers. It seems this gentleman bought a brand-new motor home with all the fancy features and drove off happily, waving out the window. Two weeks later Craig said he got a postcard saying that the customer had been in a terrible accident and had totaled his motor home. When Craig called and asked what had happened the man said, "I don't know. I was driving down the highway and I put it on cruise control. Then I went back to the kitchen to make a cup of coffee, and the next thing I knew I was in the hospital."

It made me wonder how many of us put our careers or our relationships on "cruise control" and then act shocked and surprised when we end up in traction.

I have no problem releasing others,
at least not since
I sprained my fingers.

To flatter one's self:
to
add mire.

One Halloween I had underestimated the number of children who would be coming to my door, so, after running out of candy, in desperation I began giving out quarters, nickels, and dimes. One little girl, about five years old, appeared on my doorstep dressed as a fairy princess. "I've run out of candy," I told her, dropping two quarters into her sack, "but tomorrow you can take these coins to the store and turn them into *real* candy." She slowly stepped back, gazed up at me, and said, "Look, lady, this isn't a *real* wand."

My friend Billy Bob Harris was sharing some advice his father once gave him. "He said, 'Billy Bob, you have to bring something to the table besides your appetite.'"

A friend of mine told me that Mitzi, her ten-year-old cocker spaniel, reminds her in spirit of her former mother-in-law. "She has marked out the entire world as her territory, and she keeps watch on all activities from her couch in the sunroom. She usually has a pure white sock dangling from her mouth, which she guards with ferocity. Running and playing are unforgivable acts—punishable by long, low growls—or an out-and-out pounce and attack."

Graceful giving
should be
ungainly.

My mother, Irene Jones, says,
"If you're going to fall, fall forward."

Another saying Mom has is:
"Every knock is really a boost."

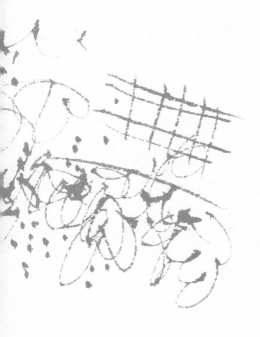

The Pond

When I lived in the forest
in what turned out to be
a lonely marriage
I went often to a little pond
on a ridge below our cabin.
One day a very fast wind blew
and caught the sparks
from a careless child's match.
The camp had to be evacuated.
Headlines the next day
stated the camp
had been destroyed.
When I returned to our cabin
I found only the plumbing standing.
I trudged from the cabin's ashes
down to the ridge—fearing what
I would find.
And yet—as if by miracle—
there stood the little pond—

shining bright and blue
with green grass all around it.
The fire had come to the edge
of the ridge and stopped.
How grateful I was for that green pond—
a tiny spot of green and blue
in a world now charcoal gray.
It made me think of other things—
like the quality of mercy—
or how even a simple thing—
like an act of kindness—
has within it hidden powers
to halt the path
of a fire.

Sometimes I wish
my ears were
tilted upward.

On a Six-Day Life Span

I wonder if butterflies
take the time at all
to sit and study
solemnly
calendars in fall.

When you get kissed in the ear
it seems the whole world must have heard.

Squiggles are laughing lines.

*A New Chinese Proverb Regarding Refusing
to Face the Facts About a Relationship*

One who eat soup
with fork
plan to stay hungry
a very long time.

I have felt God's thumb
upon me—
but never His fingernails.

If all around me
was white and warm
I'd be unhatched.

A Tree's Last Words at Oceanside

I the tree have seen the seasons
borne the winter in my branches
seen the summer surge beneath me
scattered springtime
like free green.

I and sea have sung in chorus
to the stellar host before us
in the silent bowl of evening
no one near
to clap or cheer.

All the stars have kissed my branches.
Stars are leaves on hidden trees.
You bring chainsaws now to slay me?
I could show you galaxies.

Throw My Longings Forward

Throw my longings forward
free me
from the battered mast.
Let my heart leap out
at oceans
and forget the
desert past.
Let me be like young Columbus
seeking newer, distant shores
rather than some cornered beggar
huddling by a stranger's store.

Let me feel the salt spray stinging
from the universal breast
rather than be safe and warm and dry
settling for less.

Let there be no backward glances
to a world misshaped by time.
Let there be Mariner's certainty
that all the sea
is Thine.

Let there be Explorer's confidence
carving a niche in time.
Let me call out to the galaxies—
"Today—
Tomorrow's mine!"

Sedona Sacrifice

Leave this small part of God's world,
that which is still untouched, unscarred . . .

leave it as it is.

Please, no more roads, and
smoke-belching road equipment
stirring and churning the red dirt
till when it rains . . .

Earth's blood
    runs
        down
            the
                hills

And across the roads

Like a sacrifice.

—Irene Jones

The Toolbox

I'm looking for a compartment
in the little silver toolbox
that I bought when I was ten
and kept hidden under my bed.

I'm looking for a compartment
that I can put my personal life in
to make sure it doesn't get mixed up
with my professional one.

I used to keep in that toolbox
poems that I had written
and my little blue diary
that had a golden key.
I also kept a tigereye
that Granddad had given me
and an eagle feather
I had found out in the yard.

Maybe it was a hawk feather
or another kind of feather
but certainly it wasn't a common
feather
and that's why it went in my box.
I would wait until my sister was gone
and drag out the box and look at it—
the treasures that a ten-year-old
considers highly secret.

Now I want the toolbox for a different
reason. It's become more of a money box
where I transfer funds from the top
to the bottom and then from the bottom
to the top again, and it hasn't been much fun lately
digging the toolbox from under the bed.

So I think if I can find maybe
just one more compartment
I can separate my joys
from my fears
and just get out that hawk feather
and ooh and ahhh again.

Dreams . . . They Sleep

I have some beautiful dreams . . .
they sleep—
like grasses laid down
under snowy blankets
like children at naptime
with their shoes off
like old dogs slumbering
with twitching paws
like old men
no one wants to disturb
for fear they'll have
to tend them.

I have some beautiful dreams . . .
they sleep—
like big-clawed bears
in hibernation
like a chrysalis dangling
from dead branches

like a fish
so still
hidden in the rocks
in the stream's deep, deep
wet rocks.

I have some beautiful dreams—
they sleep.

And time is the distant drummer
who is humming as he walks—
tap tap
soon it will be rap rap rap
and then it will be . . .

"No, not yet!" whispers
the Mother Spirit
who does not wish
to see slumber disturbed.

Dreams are remembered times
with God.
In slumber, they are reality . . .

So Master Time—go slower here.

I have some beautiful dreams—
they sleep
and we must not
disturb them.

Tangerines at Gold Rock Ranch

Bob came by the trailer to remind us to come see their slide show of Kenya. We thanked him and after dark made our way over. The slide show was held in a fairly large hall out at Gold Rock Ranch. The slides were surprisingly good, though Bob kept admitting, "Too many elephant shots." The crowd began oohing and ahhing at four-color photos, which caused Bob to cough and admit, "Well, that was actually a postcard that I took a picture of." Many of the slides were of tourists trying to locate the cheetah in the grass or the leopard in the tree.

Sue asked, "Do the natives always dress up like that or usually go naked?" Bob calmly replied, "I don't know. We only saw them with clothes on." And after the final elephant-shot slide we all stood up for ice cream.

Kathy and her new husband, Tom, dished it up while Miriam passed out the cookies. Miriam had a world map laid out on the pool table, and people leaned over it to locate places while they waited in line. The bulletin board posted the next Bible study as being held this Sunday at

10 A.M. Sue stuffed two handfuls of tangerines into my pocket saying, "Go ahead and take them. They're from my tree, so they're free." Dominic said in awe, "I feel like I'm on a movie set or in some kind of dream sequence— out here at Gold Rock Ranch."

The stars snuggled up to a half-grinning moon while we all walked back to our trailers—only the sound of gravel crunching under our boots warning the coyotes not to come out and play. As I walked past the broken water tower, I wondered that here in a tiny mining town twenty people had just seen Kenya, yet all seemed happy just to head back home with pockets full of tangerines. It was sort of Paradise-like, in a way. We had tasted the fruit of distant knowledge and still remained content where we were.

Showing a Friend Pictures of
Our Old Chicken Coop

This is where I first got kissed—right out by this
    doorway.
And here I used to measure myself—wanting so
    much to be five feet tall
that I'd measure with my boots on.

And here we used to keep the horses.
A Tennessee walker got a new lease on life
thanks to Dad's proven formula of epsom salts
    applied
to his torn hoof—soaking it twice a day.

We'd alternate—take turns in the morning—
letting Adam rest his head on our shoulders
while we soaked that hoof.
So many winter mornings were spent with Adam
    snoring—with me snoring with him.

The chicken coop went down one day
to make way for a tennis court.

I wish I'd kept that old doorknob, though.
It had opened up so many things—
the smell of the hay on a summer's evening . . .
the scent of a skunk who had happened by . . .
the mustiness of pigeons
who flapflapped when
you'd arrive.

Many secrets happened here.

I learned how to soap a saddle . . .
caught a baby mouse once with my bare hands
and was airlifting it to safety—
only to have our dog, Lady, grab it and swallow it
    whole.
My sister was with me at the time
and that night
whenever
Lady would burp
Kathy would shriek and hide her eyes.

The chicken coop door never did close right.
In fact—
it's not closed now.

Lost on the Lake in Canada

It started out as a calm day. I slipped into the kayak as if I had been raised on the water rather than in a distant desert town where any rare collection of moisture qualified as a lake. This is what I had come to Canada for. To be one with All That Is. I knew I would get wet.

While two of our crew headed for the horizon, I took off on my own, alternately paddling and resting, listening to the silence. Time was not relevant. All was good. I dipped my hand down into the water and watched the ripples fade away. Soon, I could not see the others. No matter. I knew where and when we said we'd meet. Drifting and dabbling for several hours, I waited until I had a good thirty minutes or so to reach my destination and then headed for the point. Only—it had moved. The landscape was unfamiliar. I paddled quickly to what I thought surely had to be the destination, only to discover that it, too, was unfamiliar.

Now the wind had picked up. I began to paddle in earnest. My arms were weakening, but I could not stop. I realized I had miles to go and time was running out. I had missed the point. I began to call up images of marathon runners who ran for four hours and more. I tried to remember times in my past when I had surprised myself and others with my physical stamina and fortitude.

Not being able to think of any, I began to sing "Zoom Golly Golly"—a camp song I had learned years ago about natives marching into the sunrise. I wondered if the words meant something like "Does anybody know where we are?" but I couldn't spend too much energy translating—or attempting to translate—a foreign song. I was lost on a lake in Canada—one of the biggest countries in the world. A country so big it covers the top half of an entire continent. I bit my lip—forcing off thoughts of fear and grizzly bears as one swats at flies . . . I wondered if they had buzzards in Canada—lake-landing buzzards attracted to blondes who were dressed in neon pink shorts and paddled in circles singing obscure African marching songs . . . songs that got weaker . . . and weaker . . .

"Jones! Jones! Snap out of it!" I said to myself, whipping my wandering mind back to reality. "You are strong. Your muscles are taut and supple . . . taut, anyway . . . You can do this. You will navigate safely to the Point

Whose Location Is No Longer Known. You will become one with your boat and you will glide swiftly and surely to shore."

The waves were higher now. I wondered when my worried friends would begin to send out the search party. I shook off thoughts of loss again and named my kayak Kiosk. "Come, Kiosk, come with me . . . guide me surely and swiftly to shore. Kiosk the Kayak knows Canada . . ." Had I read that somewhere in a travel brochure? My mind must be slipping . . . "So tragic to have perished in Canada" . . . I could see the headlines now.

And then, I heard it. A buzzing noise. A mechanical buzzing noise.

Perhaps they'd dispatched a helicopter to find me! Or a rescue hydrofoil. Maybe it was some logger felling a giant tree, who took notice of me and was signaling his fellow loggers to assist in the rescue.

The buzzing kept getting closer. I would not perish after all! I paddled with renewed energy, turning Kiosk deftly around the bend, and then there it was . . . he was. The "rescue team." A royal Canadian yuppie—mowing his lawn.

"Laurie, you weirdo! We're over here!" my friends yelled, sitting on a log eating their sandwiches. "What were you doing on that side of the lake?" Terri asked me as I pulled ashore.

"You mean you could see me the whole time?" I asked incredulously.

"Sure we could," she said, munching her sandwich, holding up her binoculars. "We just didn't know what you were doing. It looked like you were paddling in circles and singing songs to yourself."

"Oh, I wasn't doing anything really," I said. "I thought I was lost."

"Ha ha ha ha," they laughed as we loaded up the car. "Laurie thought she was lost on a lake in the middle of a golf course!"

"There's a *golf course* all around this lake?" I asked in disbelief. "But I thought you said we were in the wilderness." "No," Terri corrected me as she turned on the ignition, "I said 'we were in the rough.'"

To shepherd a flock of butterflies
one must stand there
in delight.

In stooping low and bending
to another's aid
we rise—

yet if we just live dancing
we,
too,
reach paradise.

About the Author

Laurie Beth Jones, the bestselling author of *Jesus, CEO; The Path;* and *Jesus in Blue Jeans,* is president and founder of The Jones Group, an award-winning leadership development firm. She carries out her mission "to recognize, promote, and inspire the divine connection in all of us" through her books, songs, speeches, and consulting work. She divides her time between her office in San Diego and her horse ranch in West Texas.

For more information about her work and the Jesus, CEO Foundation, contact:

Dee Jones
The Jesus CEO Foundation
813 Summersong Court
Encinitas, CA 92024
Phone: (760) 753-7251
Fax: (760) 634-2707
Website address: www.lauriebethjones.com
E-mail: laurie@lauriebethjones.com